lonely planet
Kids

WORLD'S COOLEST JOBS

ACKNOWLEDGEMENTS

Project managed by Duck Egg Blue
Author: Anna Brett
Commissioning Editor: Christina Webb
Design and Illustration: Craig and Kait Eaton
at Duck Egg Blue
Art Director: Andy Mansfield
Publishing Director: Piers Pickard
Publisher: Hanna Otero
Print Production: Lisa Taylor

Published in April 2020 by Lonely Planet Global Ltd

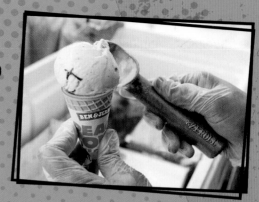

CRN: 554153
ISBN: 978 1 78868 925 0

www.lonelyplanetkids.com
© Lonely Planet 2020

Printed in Singapore
10 9 8 7 6 5 4 3 2 1

STAY IN TOUCH
lonelyplanet.com/contact

Lonely Planet Offices
AUSTRALIA The Malt Store, Level 3, 551 Swanston St., Carlton, Victoria 3053 T: 03 8379
8000
IRELAND Digital Depot, Roe Lane (off Thomas St.), The Digital Hub, Dublin D08 TCV4
USA 155 Filbert St., Suite 208, Oakland, CA 94607 T: 510 250 6400
UK 240 Blackfriars Rd., London SE1 8NW T: 020 3771 5100

Contents

Panda NANNY

Become chief cuddler of the cutest creatures around!

Giant pandas are cute and cuddly but sadly they are a rare species due to habitat loss. So at special centers in China, the birth of each new baby panda is cause for celebration. Every newborn gets a nanny to give it lots of love and care, and the best news is you can be paid $32,000 to do this!

Baby pandas are born pink, blind, and only 6 in. (15 cm) long!

SUPER CUTE!

The role of a panda nanny is to feed, clean, and care for the young pandas 24 hours a day. You'll need to be strong enough to carry lots of bamboo every day, as well as construct natural playgrounds for the pandas to exercise in.

AWWW!

GOOD TO KNOW

Hazards include the occasional scratch and bite, but the bonus is being able to live on-site, with free meals and the use of a car.

Once the pandas are a little older, you might have to wear a panda costume to interact with them. This helps to reduce human contact and get them ready for release into the wild.

JOB INFO:

SALARY: $32,000 plus meals, board, and car.

REQUIREMENTS: Writing and photography skills and "some basic panda knowledge."

COMPETITION: You might have to compete against 100,000 other applicants for this fun job.

Octopus KEEPER

Care for these clever creatures.

Grab your scuba gear—a job in an aquarium is all about helping show off amazing underwater creatures to the public. This often includes taking care of the highly intelligent octopus. These soft, squeezable mollusks like to play hide-and-seek, so octopus keepers need to stay alert at all times.

SO MANY SUCKERS!

Octopuses' tentacles connect directly to their head!

GOOD TO KNOW

In April 2016, at the National Aquarium of New Zealand, an octopus named Inky squeezed out of its tank and made a dash for a drainpipe!

The job involves caring for the octopuses by cleaning their tanks, checking the water quality, and keeping a close watch on their eggs.

The blue-ringed octopus is popular in aquariums due to its beautiful markings, but it is one of the most dangerous creatures in the sea. You'll need to avoid aggravating them when cleaning the tank as their venom is similar to the deadly poison dart frog's and will affect your ability to breathe within minutes.

Blue-ringed octopus!

COOL FACTS:

NUMBER OF SPECIES: Around 300.

COMMON FEATURES: Three hearts, eight limbs, squirt ink.

SUCKER USES: Grip, taste, and touch.

LARGEST: Giant Pacific octopus—arm span 29.5 ft. (9 m), weight 595 lb. (270 kg).

SMALLEST: Wolfi octopus—arm span 1 in. (2.5 cm), weight 0.03 oz. (1 g).

LIFESPAN: 1–2 years.

Puppy Bowl REFEREE

ANIMAL PLANET TV SHOW, US

Track this mutt match and stop fouls on the playing field.

You've heard of the Super Bowl, but what about the Puppy Bowl? Once a year, puppies from shelters compete in two teams—Team Ruff and Team Fluff—to win the sought-after chewy trophy. And keeping it all under control is the human referee (accompanied by a sloth assistant, naturally!).

There's a tinkle on the 20.

I smell an Illegal Odor Downfield.

YAP!

WOOF!

The main requirement for this job is that you love animals. But you should also be prepared to make tough decisions and keep order among the 12 dogs on the field. The show will be broadcast on TV, so you should work on your smile and presentation skills as well.

Keep these tricky pooches in line!

GOOD TO KNOW

All the dogs that compete are from shelters and need to be adopted. A perk of this job is that you might actually get to take a puppy home with you!

Snake VENOM MILKER

Get the world's most venomous snakes to bite.

Extracting venom from snakes is hugely important. The poisonous fluid can be used to treat blood clots, reduce heart attack risks, and, most importantly, create antivenom, the cure for snake bites. The difficulty is that this is a task that must be done by hand! You'll need nerves of steel as well as zoologist qualifications and training on how to handle these risky reptiles.

YIKES!

Luckily there's always antivenom on hand for snake milkers!

A snake milker doesn't work in the wild. You'll be based in a serpentarium lab at a zoo or university. To milk the snake, carefully pick it up by its head and get it to bite down on the edge of a glass covered with a thin rubber cap. The rubber pulls back a "skin" on the snake's fangs, which stimulates the venom release—just as if a snake were biting its prey. You'll need to milk thousands of times to get enough venom to send to the lab.

The fangs pierce through the rubber cap on the glass jar.

Snakes can produce between a few drops and a few teaspoons of venom when they bite.

Snakes that are milked include cobras, mambas, vipers, asps, corals, sea snakes, and rattlesnakes.

The world's most venomous snake is the inland taipan—one bite has enough venom to kill 100 people.

JOB INFO:

SALARY: $30,000 per year.

REQUIREMENTS: A degree in zoology, biochemistry, or herpetology, plus handling and identification courses.

OFFICE: Controlled serpentarium laboratory.

POTENTIAL EMPLOYERS: Universities, zoos, laboratories, pharmaceutical companies.

Sloth REHABILITATOR

Help rescue, rehabilitate, and then release.

Work at the Sloth Sanctuary in Costa Rica and you'll help look after 150 injured, orphaned, and abandoned sloths. It was the first sloth rescue center in the world, and before 1992, when the first sloth was rescued, there was little knowledge about how to care for these creatures. You'll get huge job satisfaction when you release a healthy sloth back into the wild.

The Sloth Sanctuary, Costa Rica

GOOD TO KNOW

The mission of a wildlife rehabilitator is to rescue, rehome, research, and release the animals, while educating people about the animal's natural habitat.

Many of the sloths taken to the sanctuary are young and have been separated from their mothers. Baby sloths cling to their mother's belly for a year after birth, so you'll need to act as a surrogate mother and feed them with goat's milk—the best substitute for sloth milk. The rehabilitation job also includes weighing the sloths daily and giving them baths to help improve any skin conditions. You'll also need to check their poop for any signs of malnutrition!

Keep track of every sloth's weight.

You'll study sloths to learn more about how their bodies work. For example, why are they so slow? Because it takes their systems up to a month to digest food and release the energy from it!

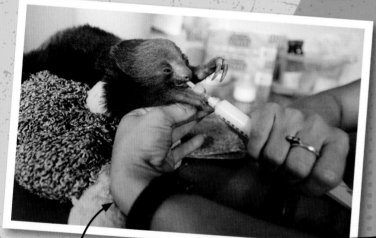

Baby sloths are fed goat's milk by the team.

Sloths can rotate their necks more than 270 degrees, which helps them feed easily in the wild.

Ostrich BABYSITTER

Keep constant watch over these feisty flightless birds.

Ostrich farming is an important industry in South Africa, and unlike calm cattle or sheep, these aggressive birds need special attention. Farmers employ people to make sure the birds don't escape, get eaten by predators, or even peck each other to death.

Ostriches can run at up to 45 mph (70 kph), so invest in some running shoes for this job.

PECK! PECK!

Ostriches can be aggressive towards each other as well as their babysitters.

The role of a babysitter starts (naturally) with the babies. Ostriches lay the largest eggs in the world—6 in. (15 cm) long and up to 3.3 lb. (1.5 kg) in weight—and they are incubated for 40 days in a communal nest. You'll need to keep a close watch. Once they hatch, the babies will be walking around within a couple of days. Then the fun really begins, as you'll have to stop them from pecking at each other—and you!

AWW!

Ostriches are fully grown at 18 months, and, as the largest birds in the world, they have a powerful kick. They are very territorial, so you'll have to help keep the peace, then get ready to start the process again with a whole new batch of eggs.

Wildlife PHOTOGRAPHER

Tell the story of the wildlife you spot.

This job is all about taking photos of wild animals in their natural habitats. But you'll also need knowledge about the animals you're photographing, as well as an understanding of the landscapes in which they live. You need to venture into remote locations and take beautiful photos of the animals even when you are very much out of your comfort zone.

You might even make a new friend!

It's your job to promote the beauty of the natural world and help to protect it.

GOOD TO KNOW

Before you move on to wild animals in exotic locations, start by photographing creatures close to home, like birds, bugs, or even your own pets!

Plan a trip to your subject's habitat. Be prepared for it to include a long journey, since many of these animals live in remote places. It's important to be in good shape, because you'll carry lots of heavy equipment! Once you arrive, you'll spend a lot of time observing your subject to understand its habits. You'll need to be patient. Sometimes it can take hours (or days!) to get just the right shot.

Photo equipment can be really heavy!

It's never too soon to start training for this career—perhaps start by taking photos in your garden or local park. You can then progress as a photographer's assistant and attend lots of talks and workshops.

It's not a glamorous job: photographers sometimes camouflage themselves to get the best shots!

CLICK
CLICK
CLICK

LEGOLAND®
MODEL MAKER

Spend your days building a world out of LEGO® bricks.

There are LEGOLAND® resorts around the world and all of them require a team of people to maintain the models and create new displays for big events. With just bricks and their brains, model makers come up with the designs and then put them together for the public to enjoy.

You can find LEGOLAND® resorts in Denmark, the UK, Germany, Japan, Malaysia, Dubai, and the US.

When you interview for this job, you'll be entered into a "brick-off" building challenge against other applicants, so practice with those blocks. You'll need some creative design experience for imagining all the model ideas, as well as knowledge of math and science for planning how to actually construct those huge models so they don't topple over.

27 x 10 BLOCKS = ?

WOW!

40 x 5 BLOCKS = ?

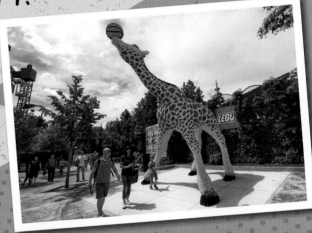

What would you look like as a Minifigure?

LEGOLAND® Windsor in the UK offers you the chance to work with a Master Builder for a day. Begin by building a figure of yourself, then learn all the techniques to create your own themed model, and go behind the scenes at the resort.

A LEGOLAND® MODEL MAKER

LEGOLAND® model maker Lucy Gullon studied television and movie set design at college and really enjoyed the model-making aspects of the course. She saw the advertisement for a model maker role at LEGOLAND® so applied and got the job at the Windsor, UK, resort!

9am The day always begins by looking over the models to check for repairs. In Windsor, there's the resort and two hotels to check.

11am You're always thinking about designing and prototyping models for future exhibits, so it's nice to sit down and play with bricks for a bit.

Even royals make it into brick form!

1pm In the afternoon, your attention shifts to building the actual models for the park and installing them. Miniland UK is made from over 42 million bricks.

4pm When building, you create stories to accompany the scene to ensure it comes to life. You might need to check details of previous real-life events for inspiration, so there is a bit of time to spend on the computer at the end of the day.

Miniland recreates famous landmarks in miniature LEGO® form and requires lots of detail to set the scene. Miniland London is filled with extras like red buses, black cabs, telephone boxes, police officers, and, if you look closely, even a LEGO® Mary Poppins!

Photos are also used as reference for the models.

21

Professional MAGICIAN

Tour the world inspiring mystery and wonder.

What does it take to become a magician? Practice and polish! And you'll need to have mastered magic tricks that will impress your audiences enough for them to pay to watch you perform. You'll need to use classic techniques but also dream up your own unique tricks—so get ready to be creative and also use logic and math to build the fantasy into reality.

Street performing is fun and a good way to build up your confidence.

WOW!

Act out your magic. It's a performing art!

There are four main areas of magic. First are sleight of hand tricks that use balls, coins, or cards to fool your audience at close range.

Stage illusions use props and lights to create large-scale magic tricks, like making a table appear to fly.

Escape tricks are where you find your way out of restraints and traps.

Finally, mind tricks involve reading audience members' minds or predicting their answers to specific questions.

GOOD TO KNOW

Magicians are self-employed so you can set your own fee. A children's birthday party might earn you $100 an hour, a stage show could earn you thousands, and an appearance on TV might make you hundreds of thousands.

ROLE MODELS

Look up these famous magicians:

Derren Brown for mind tricks,
Harry Houdini for escape tricks,
Fay Presto for sleight of hand tricks,
David Copperfield for stage illusions.

Costume DESIGNER

Play dress up every day.

Get your creative juices flowing as you bring a character to life through their clothes. Costume design is an important part of character development. You'll need to research the look of your character first. Then, get your sketchbook out and come up with a design before gathering your materials and starting to sew.

Use your imagination and a variety of objects, such as feathers, to enhance parts of your design.

Be prepared to talk to the director about the scenery as well so the clothes won't clash!

Theaters, and TV and movie sets are inspiring and creative places to work as the stories they tell feature historical characters, fantasy characters, and even animals. You'll need to think about wigs, masks, wings, and feet, as well as choosing the correct fabrics to allow the characters to move in the appropriate way.

GOOD TO KNOW

You could win an industry award for your creations. Costume designers are recognized with Tony, Academy, and Emmy awards in the US, and other countries have their own honors.

You might use your fabrics to make character props as well, like the dragon in the back of this scene.

Costume designers need to think about the flow of the play or opera. Will the actors require quick costume changes? How will they get in and out of their clothes?

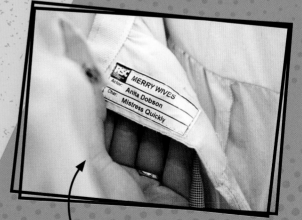

All costumes need to be labeled, as each one is made to fit the individual actor.

Special effects MAKEUP ARTIST

FILM AND TV SETS, WORLDWIDE

Make monsters and creatures come to life.

Transform a human face into a fantasy creature, a wounded victim, or even a piece of art using makeup and prosthetics (fake body parts). To really change an actor's look, you'll need to create a new 3D skin for them out of latex and then give it the right color and markings. Film studios often employ a team of special effects makeup artists to bring fantasy characters to the screen.

This lion man looks roar-some!

While some special effects can look scary, they are completely harmless!

YIKES!

26

The tools of your trade are many and varied! Of course you'll need makeup, but also brushes, puffs, and sponges to create different textures. A palette is handy for mixing the perfect color. Liquid latex is what's used to create small fake burns and cuts. It also acts as a glue for solid latex prosthetics, like fake noses. Finally, all good special effects makeup artists have a bottle of fake blood on hand.

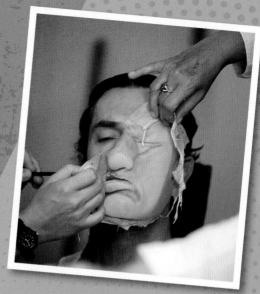

You'll most likely be a freelancer, so film and TV studios will hire you for specific projects. The best way to win this work is to build up a portfolio showing your skills. Take photos of every look you create, whether it's at home or for a job, and put them in a display folder alongside details of the work.

GOOD TO KNOW

Many artists begin with a college art course, but you can easily buy a beginner's kit and enroll in a makeup course or even follow an online tutorial.

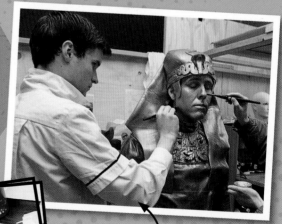

Makeup artists use a lot of different brushes!

You can also look for work in theaters, on cruise ships, at amusement parks, and even on fashion shows.

Sand SCULPTOR

Make sandcastles for a living.

This job seems pretty straightforward—just create amazing models out of sand and water. But it's harder than it looks to become the best and get paid for it! There are only 300 "master" sand sculptors in the world. To win the World Championships of Sand Sculpting or become a Guinness World Record holder can take years of hard work and training.

AWESOME WORK!

28

Sand sculptors can make money by winning competitions. They usually have less than 24 hours to complete their models. Once a sculptor has built up a reputation, they may also be hired to sculpt at events. Sand can be brought to any location and sculpted into something linked to a brand or event. An airline once paid for sculptors to create sand passengers jetting off to a beach destination as part of its marketing campaign!

Choose your sand wisely! It needs to be wet to be sticky. Heavy sand is best because it has square-shaped grains that lock together. You'll then need shovels and buckets to get started, chisels and palette knives to create the detail, and a brush or straw to remove loose grains.

GOOD TO KNOW

Look into joining the WSSA (the World Sand Sculpting Academy). It's a network of professional sand artists.

29

London Dungeon ACTOR

Terrify people through hundreds of years of history.

The Dungeons whisk visitors back in time to London's dark past, when characters of the city were not always pretty. As an actor here you might play Guy Fawkes, the executioner at the Tower of London, a plague doctor, or even Jack the Ripper. In fact, actors often play around 15 parts in 19 different shows each week.

SUPER SCARY!

You'll need to stay in character at all times—remember, the visitors are prepared to be scared!

For this job, you'll need to learn about all the characters by doing background research, because they're based on fact, not fiction. They may all have a different accent and historical contexts, so your memory needs to be sharp to keep each role distinct. You'll be part of a small cast of around 20 actors entertaining audiences of up to 45 at a time. This is fast-paced interactive drama that is not for the fainthearted!

You may sometimes need to tone down your character for young children, or add extra horror for those looking bored!

You should learn to improvise as well. This is the art of acting without a script, so you can react to what is happening around you at that moment while staying in character.

You'll often be working in low lighting, so get to know your way around the sets and acclimatize yourself to the blood and gore in some scenes.

Children's book ILLUSTRATOR

Bring ideas to life through art.

You can tell a story by speaking to others or writing it down, and having artwork to accompany it adds another level of enjoyment for those reading it. Children's book illustrators are able to communicate stories and depict scenes in picture form using a wide variety of techniques, from pencils to digital collage.

Use a sketchbook to get your initial ideas down on paper.

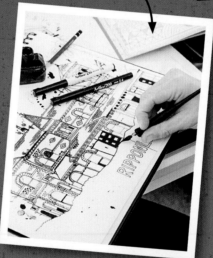

You may be asked to draw text for a book cover as well as the illustrations.

Being able to draw is a key requirement of this job. But you may also choose to work using sculpture or digital art, so don't worry if you're not a still-life specialist. You do need to be able to communicate your ideas though, so that if someone asks for a character, you have lots of options ready to put down on the page.

GOOD TO KNOW

Although you'll create your art alone, you also need to be able to work on a team. You may need to communicate with an art director, writer, and editor when working on a book.

While you get to make art all day long, you do need someone to pay you to do this! You're a one-person business, so take steps such as building a website, getting set up with an agency, or e-mailing ideas to book publishers. You may be asked to develop your own book, but more likely you'll be given a brief from a client. This gives an idea of what images they need you to create, but it's up to you to sketch out options and then tweak them again and again following feedback to end up with artwork everyone is happy with.

Sometimes it helps to sketch out different ideas before you work on final illustrations.

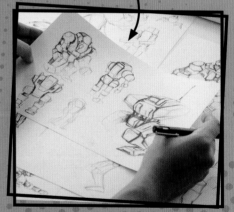

Using a computer, a designer will position your artwork alongside the text.

Once your sketches are approved, it's time to make them real. Put your pencils, paints, or other materials to work, and then scan your images onto a computer so you can send them electronically. All commercial books need to exist in digital form, so learning how to use the right computer programs is worth the effort.

A DAY IN THE LIFE OF

AN ILLUSTRATOR

James Gulliver Hancock is an illustrator who's created artwork for books, museums, and even animations. He draws almost every day, and has done since childhood. After studying visual communications, he set himself up as an illustrator for hire. He has his own personal projects, and clients around the world who want to use his illustration style on their projects.

7am Working for clients around the world means e-mails arrive at all times of day, so the first thing to do is check to see what's arrived overnight. This might mean feedback on a sketch, or a new piece of work that's urgent, so once I've been through everything, I can make my to-do list for the day.

9am I have a studio at home, so I move into here and get my pencils and paper out. The mornings are always spent drawing, and I like to listen to podcasts while I do so. I have various projects on the go at the same time and they are often at different stages, but I try and focus on one thing at once.

One of James's books, *How Cities Work*, explores the inner workings of a modern city, with flaps to lift and pages to unfold.

1pm I like to go outdoors after lunch to get some fresh air and clear my head. I'll then head back to the studio and use the afternoon to work on the computer. I have a scanner, so I can turn my paper art into digital form and sharpen up any lines or colors using a program called Adobe Illustrator.

GOOD TO KNOW

One of my personal projects was to draw many of the buildings in New York City. It made me draw every day and was like keeping a visual diary of where I'd been.

4pm Children's books often take six months to create, so there's lots of stopping and starting while I wait for the next brief to arrive, or for comments to be returned on my sketches. I often fill these gaps with "quick" jobs, like some art for a newspaper article that needs to be completed in two days.

8pm If I have a free evening, I'll continue working on my own projects, like drawing the things around me. I upload these onto my website, and with any luck, a client will spot them and they can form the basis of a new project.

Foley SOUND ARTIST

FOLEY RECORDING STUDIOS, WORLDWIDE

Create sound effects every way imaginable.

The job of a Foley sound artist is rare to find but very cool. You need to give what you see on-screen an accurate sound representation in the post-production stage of a movie. You'll create all kinds of noises, from the swishing of windshield wipers to the shattering of glass to the clomping of horses' hooves.

GOOD TO KNOW

This job is named after Jack Foley, the first sound effects artist who specialized in this area.

You'll need to watch the movie in slow motion to make your sound effect at exactly the right second.

Start out in this career with a background in audio production or recording arts. If you're lucky enough to work in a purpose-built Foley studio, you'll be surrounded by thousands of props—otherwise, collect your own. Microphones capture the sound, and a mixer will work in a studio next to you to mix and layer the individual sounds. You need to be very accurate matching the timing and strength of these noises to what is seen on-screen.

SPLAT!

The fun part of this job is thinking outside the box. Use coconut shells for hoof noises, and frozen lettuce for a good crunching noise. You'll also need to use a pool for aquatic sounds and floor space covered in different materials.

The effects are recorded and edited on a huge sound-mixing desk!

SO MANY BUTTONS!

Motion capture ACTOR

Let your movements be the starring role.

Ever wondered how Gollum in *Lord of the Rings* and Kong in *King Kong* looked so realistic? It's thanks to actors who played them, and the motion capture teams behind it all. Branch off into the digital realm of acting, and you'll not be typecast into a role based on the way you look. Instead, you'll create a digital character through the way that you move.

GOOD TO KNOW

You'll work with the wider pre-production team in a fast-paced environment where the results are required to be flawless.

The motion capture suit is wireless and specially designed to allow the actor to move freely.

Motion capture works by recording your body movements and facial expressions through sensors stuck onto your body or a special suit. A wireframe skeleton based on you is then created on-screen and skin, hair, and any special features are added digitally until the character comes to life. Its digital movements follow your unique real-life movements, which makes for a very realistic end result.

The industry is growing as computer games also require mo-cap actors. It helps to be good at martial arts moves for these projects!

A number of colleges worldwide now offer motion capture courses in their animation degrees. This is for those people who want to be behind the camera. You'll need to be good on a computer for this role so you can transfer the movements you film into the digital artwork.

COOL OUTFIT!

Video
GAME DESIGNER

Design and create a completely new world.

The video game industry is huge, and makes a lot of money! All those gamers out there are just waiting for new material to appear—on consoles, computers, and phones. As a game designer, it's up to you to dream up the extraordinary and turn it into a game people can interact with.

Discuss your ideas with team members to get further inspiration.

Players now like to record and livestream their play, especially at tournaments, so you can watch how gamers explore your creation!

RAW render

There are many aspects to game design: designers look at the story concept, the puzzle aspect, and individual levels; animators create the visual details, including characters; programmers code the game so it flows seamlessly. There's an extensive testing phase at the end, too.

Computer games first became popular in the 1970s when games like Space Invaders got players hooked.

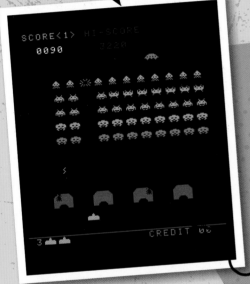

Today, virtual reality games are the latest development.

GOOD TO KNOW

Software application developers are said to earn around $98,000 a year.

You should be interested in 3D digital art, although it doesn't hurt to be able to draw with a pencil. Animation degrees, computer engineering, or game design courses are all a good training ground.

A designer creates a 3D character for inclusion in the game.

Hot-air BALLOON PILOT

THE SKY IS YOUR OFFICE

A job that allows you to be on cloud nine.

As a commercial balloon pilot, you'll fly sky high, feeling as free as a bird—and you'll get paid to take others with you. You might take part in competitions, fly tourists around, or display advertisements on your balloon, but on every trip you'll find moments of calm as you quietly drift along with the wind.

FLY HIGH!

A burner heats up the air inside the balloon, which causes it to rise.

RA–0940G

РУСБАЛ

To qualify for the job you'll need to attend hot-air balloon school. The first requirement is to obtain your private pilot's license, then your balloon certificate, after which you can train with a commercial instructor. You might be lucky to complete this within three months, but if you want to fly above certain heights, you'll need more experience. You need to master a smooth landing if you want to keep your customers happy, too!

A successful landing!

Hot-air balloons come in all shapes and sizes!

In our modern-day busy skies, you'll always need to check airspace restrictions, flight rules, and emergency procedures. This job is suitable for people who are skilled at working methodically.

This job allows you to travel the world. You could run commercial flights over popular places like the Serengeti in Africa.

GOOD TO KNOW

Join your national ballooning federation to find out more about hot-air ballooning.

Dinosaur PALEONTOLOGIST

FOSSIL SITES, MUSEUMS AND LABS, WORLDWIDE

Discover animals that were previously unknown.

A paleontologist studies fossils to learn about life on Earth in the past. Of course, the role every kid wants to take on is a dinosaur specialist, but you can also build a career researching ancient plants, bacteria, and fungi. Be prepared to get dirty, because you need to dig to find the fossils!

See if you're interested in working as a paleontologist by joining a dig.

You could also volunteer at a local museum for further experience.

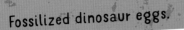

Dinosaurs ruled the world for 170 million years but are now extinct. The only way to learn about them is to look at the clues they've left behind. In the field, you'll collect fossil samples of bones, eggs, and even footprints. You've hit the jackpot if you uncover a complete skeleton. You then need to examine the samples in a lab, carefully recording the details and preserving them as you go. Finally, you can write about your findings to educate others about these prehistoric beasts.

Dino footprints have been preserved in the ground.

You need a scientific background to become a paleontologist. It's a competitive field, and many people have PhDs in their chosen area, so you'll need to study hard. You should be curious and have detailed observational skills, and you can start young by reading all about the dinosaurs that we have already discovered.

GOOD TO KNOW

Diego Suarez was just seven years old when he discovered a new dinosaur in Chile. It was named *Chilesaurus diegosuarezi* after him!

A fossil of *Ichthyosaur*.

VOLCANOLOGIST

Take notes as Mother Nature puts on a show.

Volcanologists study how and why volcanoes form, and the impact they have when they erupt. Obviously, it's incredible to watch lava spewing out of a crater and a huge ash cloud blanketing the sky, but this job is as important as it is exciting. The more you know about volcanoes, the better equipped you are to protect people from harm when they erupt unexpectedly.

SUPER HOT!

Most people run from erupting volcanoes, but your job is to watch and collect samples. Just don't risk it for that extra lump of lava!

There are around 1,500 potentially active volcanoes worldwide, so dust off your passport and be prepared to travel.

It's not just the lava that is of interest. Smoke and ash can have a huge impact on air traffic and cause nasty pollution.

To land this cool job, you'd better have a love of science and a degree in geology. You'll need to be a risk-taker but also a safety guru so you can collect those samples. Then expect to spend time in a laboratory to study your findings afterwards.

Ash clouds can travel thousands of feet up into the sky.

There are five volcano observatories in the US where you can study the country's 169 active volcanoes. The knowledge gained from this research has real-time benefits to people and governments, especially when warnings can be given before an eruption takes place.

This volcanologist is studying volcanic data from Mount Vesuvius in Italy.

A DAY IN THE LIFE OF
A VOLCANOLOGIST

A typical day for a volcanologist is in one of two locations—either in the lab, analyzing samples and monitoring live data, or out in the field, studying the volcano firsthand. It can be dangerous, so you'll need to be careful when working on the ground!

Dress in layers. It may be cold high up on a volcano, but the lava will be hot.

6am You'll wake up when the sun rises. Towns are (quite sensibly!) not usually built near volcanoes, so your accommodation is likely to be a tent. Be prepared to call this home for couple of months!

8am The weather is good so you start early by hiking up to the crater and observing, photographing, taking notes, and sampling the lava from previous eruptions. Check to see if there is a change in the height of the crater floor, as this might tell you something is happening below.

The volcano is beginning to erupt! You carefully make it back down to camp, watching out for falling rocks. Now's the time to fly the drone over the crater to get an aerial view and measure the temperature with a thermal camera.

Earthquake specialists will monitor seismograph readings for Earth tremors around the volcano.

4pm The eruption happened. Luckily, it was only small, but you still share your data with earthquake and tsunami teams in case the eruption triggers a chain of other events.

5pm You carefully head towards the line of cooling lava and take some samples. The lab will analyze the chemical composition of them to find out what depth they came from. You wear a gas mask to protect your lungs from any newly erupted volcanic gases.

7pm It's dusk, and with that your working day ends. You've had to carry all your supplies with you to camp, so you cook dinner with your colleagues before you head back to your tent to sleep.

GOOD TO KNOW

Sometimes you may need to hire a helicopter to fly you to inaccessible areas of a volcano. It's a treat to be up in the air, but very dangerous as you'll be dropped in a remote area that could be engulfed in lava at a moment's notice.

Drone PILOT

BUZZ!

THE GREAT OUTDOORS

Fly your toy all day long.

Become a drone pilot, and you'll find that your work is very varied. You could use your drone to capture images of remote places and sell the photographs, take aerial footage of sporting events, snap photos of homes and buildings for sale, or use your bird's-eye view to create maps.

Take photos of urban areas for technical work...

...or natural wonders to sell to magazines.

You'll need to invest money to get started—drones range in price from $1,000 to $120,000. To work commercially, you'll also need your remote pilot's license and specialized training, in areas like thermal photography, if you want to bid for technical work. The good news is that construction firms, real estate agents, and insurance companies all require drone imagery for their survey work, inspection jobs, or disaster relief.

Some drones can even deliver vital medical supplies!

If you work as a full-time pilot and build up a reputation, your jobs may start flooding in. But watch out—as drones increase in popularity, you'll soon have more competition.

GOOD TO KNOW

Beware of the weather—it's not easy to fly or get decent images in a storm, although some companies will pay for footage taken during a hurricane.

Flying your drone to complete the photographic part of the job might take a few hours or a day, but then comes the hard work. You'll usually be required to write a report detailing everything you've seen.

Mars ROVER DRIVER

Drive a real-life robot over uncharted land.

Do you dream of exploring far-off worlds, but don't fancy the risk that comes with blasting into space? Then working at the NASA (National Aeronautics and Space Administration) Jet Propulsion Lab might be your dream job. You'll plan exploration routes for Mars rovers, such as Curiosity, and then drive it!

★ ★ The cost to get this vehicle to Mars was $2.5 billion, so no pressure not to crash it!

✩ ✩

COSMIC FUN!

Software updates are tried out on test rovers in the lab.

There are huge power cables for the test rovers, but the rover on Mars has its own power source.

There are full-sized, functional rovers in the lab for you to test before you drive the real thing. The testing facility is also specially equipped with soil and rocks that mimic the Martian terrain, so you can recreate any obstacles encountered on Mars.

The team can work on small parts of the test rover to figure out how to fix any problems on the real thing.

Driving a machine on another planet is not easy! There's a lag of between 4 and 20 minutes in time between when the instructions are sent and when the rover receives them. Because you can't drive in real-time, the rover will sleep while you plan and then "drive" when you're off-duty. If something goes wrong, you won't know about it until the next day.

Tools at the end of Curiosity's arm

Curiosity has a robotic arm that can drill through or scoop up rock samples. Your job is to also safely operate the arm and deposit the samples into the analysis instruments on the rover.

NASA ASTRONAUT

Become one of less than 350 people to have ever done this job.

If you want to be an astronaut, you've got to be patient! The selection process takes almost two years, and then there are at least two years of training before you qualify. That's not including the degree you need to have to apply for the job. But it's worth it. Imagine getting to look down at Earth and see its curvature as you zip around it at 5 mi. (8 km) per second.

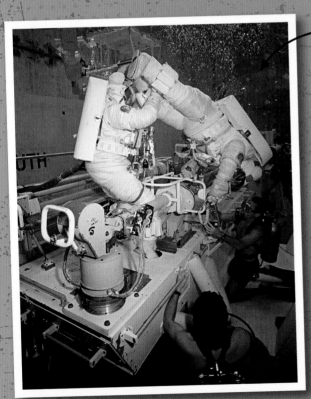

Some training takes place underwater to mimic the weightlessness experienced in space.

SPLASH!

To even be able to apply to NASA, you need a degree in an engineering, science, or math field, three or more years of professional work experience (or pilot experience), plus the fitness to pass a physical test. If you're selected, you'll need to learn to scuba dive and speak Russian, as well as complete the astronaut training.

Become a mission specialist, and you may get to visit the International Space Station (ISS). You'll be in space for up to two weeks on short missions, but a stint on the ISS will probably last six months. You may be responsible for medical or engineering experiments on board, and, as an engineer, chances are you'll get to spacewalk—the outside of the space station needs as much attention as the inside!

How tall are you? NASA requires astronauts to be between 4 ft. 10 in. and 6 ft. 3 in. so you can fit inside a space suit!

GOOD TO KNOW

Only a small class of under 50 astronauts are selected from the original 18,000 applicants. If you work for NASA, you'll be a federal employee, and your salary will be between $53,000 and $116,000.

SPACE WALK!

A DAY IN THE LIFE OF
AN ASTRONAUT

The International Space Station orbits the Earth 16 times in 24 hours, so you may think you have 16 sunrises to start the day at your leisure. But in reality, there's lots of work to be done, so the crew is woken by mission control and spends an Earth-length day at work every day.

European Space Agency astronaut, Tim Peake.

6am You're woken up by an alarm in your small sleep station. Time to float out of your sleeping bag and brush your teeth, which is a little different when in zero gravity. You'll need to swallow the toothpaste when you're done!

8am Time to put in a call to mission control to discuss the day's schedule. There are household chores and maintenance jobs to do. All the tasks have been carefully written down step by step by the team at mission control. Be careful not to lose things. Everything needs to be secured to the walls or it will float away.

Everyday items are secured to the walls by fasteners or clips.

10am Hit the gym... for two hours. Zero gravity affects your bones, and you'll lose muscle strength because you move so effortlessly, so the gym is a requirement, not a choice.

12:30pm You're working on your own experiments so won't normally stop to eat lunch with the rest of the crew, unless it's Sunday. Eating in space means adding hot water to your dehydrated packet of food to make it edible.

2pm The main reason you've been sent to live on the ISS is to conduct scientific research, so you'll work on your experiments in the lab in the afternoon. You could be studying the effects of zero gravity on materials or on living creatures like the fish and ants you brought on board with you.

8pm After dinner, there's free time to call home or watch a movie. Maybe you want to spend some time looking down on planet Earth as well before settling down to sleep again.

57

Ethical HACKER

Hack into a computer network with the blessing of your boss.

Big companies and government agencies are constantly afraid of their systems being hacked and their secrets being leaked. The only way to prevent people breaking through the security walls is to get there first! So these organizations employ "white-hat" hackers like you to find their weaknesses and fix them, before external "black-hat" hackers with criminal intent get there.

Using multiple screens allows you to run a program and check for hacks at the same time.

58

To do this job you'll need a computer programming degree and problem-solving skills. You can learn all about the latest cybersecurity threats and earn an ethical hacker certification by training with the EC-Council. Established in 2003, it's the program of choice for the US Department of Defense.

New worms, malware, viruses, and ransomware are created every day, and so the game changes all the time. Keep asking yourself the questions: What vulnerabilities do I see? What information does the hacker want to access? How can I fix the problem?

GOOD TO KNOW

You'll be paid good money, close to $100,000, because companies have to trust you to resist making extra money by selling their secrets to the highest bidder.

You may end up defending national security by preventing data from getting into the hands of terrorists.

Formula 1
PIT STOP CREW

Complete your job in three seconds flat.

Being an F1 driver might seem like the headline-grabbing job here, but the pit stop crew has some of the most thrilling and adrenaline-fueled roles in the whole team. It should take less than three seconds to change all four tires on an F1 car—are you up to the job?

Being on the tour circuit requires long-haul travel around the world and working anti-social hours to prep for a race.

Changing a tire takes only a matter of seconds, so you'll also play another role within the team. The majority of pit stop crew members are also mechanics. The chief mechanic is head of the pit crew, overseeing the changing of tires and controlling the release of the car once the pit stop is safely completed.

To become a car mechanic, you begin with an apprenticeship along with your formal training. You'll have to work your way up to Formula 1, so try and start work in junior racing. You could get involved with a team, or just help out at your local circuit on race days. Some mechanics start their careers in the military and then transition to F1.

Tires are heated in hot "blankets" before use to give them extra grip on the track.

Pit tools

The Red Bull team changed all four tires on the car in 1.88 seconds in 2019!

WOW!

Artisan CHOCOLATIER

Create the chocolate of your dreams.

Does your mouth water at the thought of chocolate? Are you a fan of fancy flavors as well as ordinary chocolate bars? Take up a career as a chocolatier, and you'll get to make your favorite treats all day long! This job requires you to be half-chef, half-business owner, especially if you want to create your own brand to sell to others.

TOTALLY YUMMY!

You'll need a steady hand for the decorating!

You'll also probably need a license and health department inspection before you can sell your products to the public.

Begin by attending a culinary school to earn a degree in pastry and baking, or try working for a chocolate manufacturer. You could also specialize with an online course in chocolate from Ecole Chocolat. When you're ready to start your own brand, remember that chocolate can be temperamental, and you'll be competing with international favorites, so there's lots to prepare before you begin.

Will you start with cocoa beans or buy blocks of chocolate from baking suppliers and then add your flavor?

Can you work from home, or do you need to rent a commercial kitchen? Either way, you'll need the pots and pans to melt the chocolate and temper it, then a thermometer, molds, and space to store it, not forgetting those extra ingredients or flavors. You'll also require packaging so customers can take their treats home.

The best part of this job is tasting your creations to find the perfect flavor!

Ben & Jerry's
FLAVOR GURU

Invent a new ice-cream flavor.

This job requires you to taste all the best foods from around the world, then figure out how they can be mixed into an ice-cream flavor. It's a tasty business to be in! Ben & Jerry's is one of the world's most innovative ice-cream makers, and nothing is off-limits in the development kitchen. Will your new funky flavor be as popular as cookie dough or fudge brownie?

New flavors are often tested in small batches. Bonnaroo Buzz (light coffee and malt ice cream with whiskey caramel swirls and toffee pieces) was introduced at a festival in 2010.

All Ben & Jerry's ice creams begin as a base of either sweet white cream or dark chocolate. You can then add purees, flavor extracts, or maybe a dash of alcohol. Stir in your chunks of cookie, fruit... or even something savory. Finish with a swirl of caramel or something similar. Then comes the hard part—think of a witty name for your creation!

The colorful entrance to the Ben & Jerry's factory

There's a lot of paperwork to do along with the taste testing. You'll need to decide where to source your ingredients, as well as manage the costs and confirm all the manufacturing details for your new flavor. Making your batches consistent in taste is also very important, and you'll need to run a quality assurance check on every batch before it gets sent out of the door.

Not all ideas pass the test—pepperoni, macaroni, and jalapeno flavors didn't make the cut! Sugar Plum was retired to the flavor graveyard after a year.

JOB INFO:

REQUIREMENTS:

1. A food science degree and around three years' experience in the food manufacturing industry.

2. A passion for ice cream and new product development.

3. Some very good taste buds!

Molecular GASTRONOMIST

Turn the experience of food upside down and inside out.

In this job you're a chef, but not in the traditional sense. You need to think outside the box and create dishes with unexpected contrasts, then use scientific tools to achieve the end result. Your food has to work for all five senses, not just taste, and also involve an element of surprise.

This molecular gastronomist has created a dish called smoking fruit soup.

GOOD TO KNOW

Molecular gastronomists often play with our sense of sight by making a sweet-looking dish out of savory flavors.

WOW!

You can now gain a degree in molecular gastronomy from a few institutions around the world, such as a masters from SOAS in London, a BA from the University of Valencia in Italy, or an MSc from Queen Margaret University in Edinburgh, Scotland. You'll learn to experiment, from using carbon dioxide to add bubbles to flash freezing with liquid nitrogen. You can even master a method called spherification, in which you'll turn liquids into small balls filled with juice.

Listen to seagulls and waves while you eat the dish Sound of the Sea.

Snail porridge!

If you get a job at Heston Blumenthal's restaurant The Fat Duck, in England, you'll be one of 42 chefs. That's one per customer! You might be involved in making nitro-scrambled egg and bacon ice cream, snail porridge, and a dish called Sound of the Sea, which incorporates sound with seafood bites. With such unexpected dishes, the food has to be perfect every time, and you'll need to maintain 100 percent concentration.

Meat fruit–pate shaped like a satsuma.

Enjoyment of food is affected by your mood. Eating a white-chocolate playing card filled with jam will always make you smile!

67

Waterslide TESTER

Slip and slide, then review the splash.

As a waterslide tester, you're responsible for the enjoyment of swimmers worldwide. A good waterslide needs strong water flow, a fun ride, and a big splash, and companies like SplashWorld resorts take this very seriously! If you're up to the task of slipping down over 150 slides and pushing your adrenalin to the max, this is the job for you.

To apply for the job, send in an application video to the company that owns the slides, explaining why you like to slide. If you're invited to an assessment day, you'll have an interview, take written tests, and perform in front of a camera to capture your presentation skills. If you reach the finals, you might be flown to a resort for a water park challenge!

Not all slides are scary—lazy river rides allow you to float along on a tube.

With flumes, lazy rivers, rapids, and vertical drops to test, be prepared to get wet. And you can't be scared of heights or get queasy at a twist or turn. Another job requirement is that you film your slides using a head camera. Once you're back in dry clothes, edit your video, and upload your review for others to see.

GOOD TO KNOW

This is an all-weather job—could you strip down to your swimwear even when it's chilly outside?

The Kilimanjaro waterslide in Brazil is the highest in the world, at 164 ft. (50 m).

69

Sydney Harbour Bridge
CLIMB LEADER

The bridge is your office.

Spend your days outdoors climbing one of the most iconic bridges in the world, and share in the excitement of a once-in-a-lifetime experience with your customers. Your job is to lead 14 people to the top of the Sydney Harbour Bridge, and then get them safely back down again.

GREAT VIEW!

GOOD TO KNOW

A typical climb takes 3.5 hours and includes over 1,400 steps. As a climb leader, you might do up to three climbs in a day.

This isn't a 9 to 5 job. Some mornings you'll be up at 3:30 to lead a sunrise climb, or be working after dark for the sunset shift.

The only qualification you need to apply for this job is a warm and friendly personality. And you'd better not be afraid of heights! You'll be put on a 2–3 week training program if you get through the interviews, and then you're ready to climb. Just make sure you're able to carry around 13 lb. (6 kg) of safety equipment, and learn to project your voice so that all 14 members of your group can hear you.

You need to wear a harness at all times when climbing.

You'll also have to be prepared to climb in all conditions, as it's only high winds or lightning storms that will keep you grounded.

Tropical island CARETAKER

Be a walking advertisement for amazing island life.

The state of Queensland in Australia ran a recruitment campaign for "the best job in the world": caretaker of a beautiful island in the Great Barrier Reef. To get the job, you had to compete against 34,000 applicants, but imagine waking up every day with the sound of the sea calling you to work! Keep an eye out for more jobs like this on islands around the world.

GOOD TO KNOW

This is a job in tourism, so after your island stint, you'll be well qualified to continue working in the tourism industry.

Ben Southall got the job on Hamilton Island!

Step one of the Hamilton Island recruitment process was an application video. If you were selected, you then had to undertake personality tests, demonstrate your blogging skills, and pass a swimming course. If you reached the final 16, you were flown to the island for four days of activities and interviews. In 2009, Ben Southall from the UK was the "winner" of this totally tropical task!

JOB INFO:

SALARY: AU$150,000

BONUS: Three-bedroom luxury villa and a golf cart to drive around the island.

JOB DESCRIPTION: Explore everything on the island, and off it, and write a blog to promote the area.

The final 16 candidates for the 2009 role.

To do this job and others like it, you have to be adventurous and outgoing so you can make friends with the locals, but also grounded so you don't mistake the island lifestyle for a vacation. There's lots of walking and swimming to do, so make sure you're physically fit. And because all islands are surrounded by water, you'd better like sea creatures!

Just moments from the island you can snorkel on the Great Barrier Reef.

Airline PILOT

Soar through the skies and see the world.

As the pilot of a huge commercial aircraft, you're able to lift over 500 people up into the air and whizz them around the globe. This is a job that sounds like magic but is open to everyone as long as you train hard, are prepared for the responsibility, and have a good head for heights.

The view from your office is impressive!

Airlines will sometimes advertise for potential pilots to apply to join their training programs. If you're selected, you'll undergo 18 months of tuition. This includes learning how the systems work and flying in simulators as well as actual time in the air.

The length of your workday depends on the distance you are flying!

74

A lot of preparation is required to do your job each day. You'll probably be given a schedule by the airline, which indicates where you are flying, but then it's up to you to research the weather at home, along the route, and at the destination. You'll also need to calculate how much fuel to carry... then make sure to add a little extra! As the passengers board, methodically go through all the checks to see that the systems are working normally. Check in with the rest of the crew, and then you can begin the flight.

Air traffic controllers act as your colleagues on the ground.

Gustaf III Airport on the island of Saint Barthélemy in the Caribbean has one of the world's shortest runways.

Takeoff and landing are the most complex parts of the role. If the weather is bad or the wind is strong, it can be tricky to navigate a plane onto the runway. When cruising high in the sky, the key is to keep the ride smooth and enjoyable for all on board. You'll also complete the paperwork and write up a report about the flight.

Stunt PERFORMER

Make danger your middle name.

Jump off a bridge onto a moving train, survive a flaming inferno, land safely after being pushed off a building—these things might not happen in real life, but they sure do in the movies! As a stunt performer, it's your job to act out these dangerous scenarios, and make sure all the safety provisions are in place, of course.

Being afraid makes you concentrate, so it's good to have a little fear of each stunt.

Judo, gymnastics, trampolining, cycling, and horseback riding are all good sports to help you practice your stunt moves.

WOAH!

There are no training courses to become a stunt performer, so work experience is a must. To help you get the work, join your country's stunt register. You'll need to demonstrate a high level of skill in fighting, riding, driving, falling, swimming, strength, and agility, as well as work as an extra or observer on a TV or movie set so you know what the industry is like. You can then work as a probationary stunt performer under the supervision of a coordinator for the first few years, before going it alone or even coordinating stunts later down the line.

Practice makes perfect... but it also helps to know people in the industry! Maybe you'll specialize in martial arts stunts so people know who to call if they are filming that type of scene.

Stunt festivals are good places to show off your skills.

GOOD TO KNOW

The more dangerous the stunt, the more money you are paid. You could earn up to $100,000 a year if you're kept busy.

Ice ARTIST

Get paid to create art that will then vanish.

For five months of the year, ice hotels in northern countries attract visitors from around the world to stay in their rooms. They need ice artists to hand-sculpt the ice suites, so this will keep you busy in winter. During the warmer months of the year, you can find work sculpting ice for festivals and events, or even making pieces for restaurants.

BRRR!

The fact that your ice sculpture is temporary makes it unique.

To become an ice artist for a hotel, submit your idea for an ice suite. A jury will select around 50 artists and then as soon as the temperature gets cold enough, it's time to relocate and start sculpting. Work quickly and with precision, as ice hotels are only standing for a few months. For all ice sculptures, decide on your ice "color" in advance; tap water will become cloudy when it freezes, but river water that freezes slowly will stay clear.

Use chainsaws, chisels, rotary tools, and files to create your art, and remember to wear gloves!

To build rooms or a giant sculpture in winter, large ice blocks are often gathered from nearby rivers and then stuck together with water. For smaller sculptures, you can freeze your own blocks of ice, but you'll need to keep it in subzero temperatures at all times during transportation.

Many ice sculptors make designs all year round for display in restaurants or at events.

You need to be able to sculpt the ice, so your qualifications for this job include being a theater, structural, or interior designer, or a ceramicist or sculptor.

Professional SLEEPER

Don't fall asleep on the job!

Yes, that's right, you can be paid to sleep! Scientists need people to test sleep-related products, furniture stores need to test their latest mattress and bed designs, and even NASA wants people to lie in bed for 70 days to replicate what happens to an astronaut's body in space.

 ZZZ!

ZZZ!

GOOD TO KNOW

The Museum of Contemporary Art in New York City paid people $10 an hour to take sleeping pills and sleep on a bed in the middle of an art exhibit.

One mattress company held a promotional event in New York and allowed people to nap in a cubbyhole. This is a good way to see if you can sleep during the day!

80

Sleep is not the only skill required for this job. Most employers need you to have good health and fitness and a personality type that doesn't mind being alone. You need the ability to sleep in new surroundings, sometimes with wires attached to you so you can be monitored. After your sleep, you will be required to review your experience and write a report.

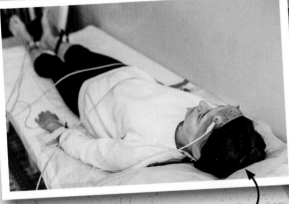

How much you'll get paid for your Z's varies. NASA paid people $18,000 to lie in a bed for 70 days back in 2013. And in 2006, hotel chain Travelodge hired a director of sleep for $73,000 to sleep in 17,000 of their rooms and evaluate comfort and surroundings.

Scientists monitor the way your brain works while you sleep. Your brain remains active, storing memories from the day and allowing you to dream.

Data such as your heart rate and breathing patterns will be recorded and analyzed by scientists to determine how well you slept. This information is then shared with the company that hired you.

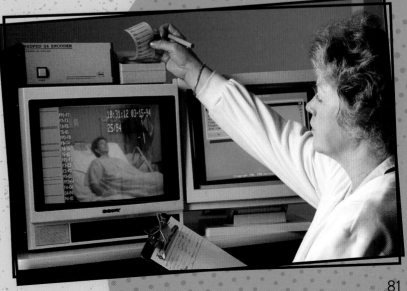

Oshiya
TRAIN PUSHER

TOKYO, JAPAN

For once it's OK to push and shove.

In Tokyo, around 20 million people take the train... every day! Even though trains run every few minutes, no one wants to be late in the busy morning rush hour. Your job is to push and pack people into the carriages so that people can get to work on time!

Some trains are filled to double their capacity!

When everyone is on board, let the driver know the train can safely depart.

SQUEEZE IN!

Oshiyas were first introduced at one of Tokyo's busiest stations: Shinjuku. It was originally a part-time job, usually done by students. But now there are regular staff members who fulfill the role. So to become an *oshiya*, you need to work for Tokyo Metro, Toei Subway, or Japan Rail and be based at a busy station. Work the morning shift to have the most people to push!

The trains in Tokyo have always been busy. This photo was taken in 1967!

Although you are pushing, your job is to also ensure the safety of passengers and make sure clothes and bags don't get caught in the doors. You are then responsible for signaling to the driver that it's OK for the train to depart. But in Japan, if a train is more than five minutes late to its destination, you'll have to apologize to the passengers and issue a delay certificate for them to show their employers.

Once you've got experience as an *oshiya* in Tokyo, you can also find pushing work in Beijing, Madrid, and Frankfurt.

Mystery SHOPPER

Shop till you drop.

With this job, you are the secret service of the shopping world. Your role, if you choose to accept it, is to review your in-store experience without being caught! You won't get any special treatment, and you'll need to keep your identity under wraps, but if you can help a store improve, then it's worth it.

To become a mystery shopper, sign up with a registered company. They post jobs online, and you can apply to win the work for a store in your area, or a supplier that interests you. You'll then need to spend an hour or more in the store, taking note of the appearance and cleanliness, the time you spend waiting in the line to pay, and the helpfulness of the staff.

If you can secretly film inside the store, you may be paid more.

84

You might be given a small amount of money to make a purchase, or you'll be reimbursed for your transportation and accommodation if you need to stay away from home. But the company will only pay once you've submitted your report. Make sure to write up your notes as soon as you can so you don't forget any details.

Try mystery dining as well. You'll get a free meal but will need to memorize every single detail because you can't write anything down in front of the waitstaff.

You review is important for independent stores as they compete with online shopping.

Tower of London RAVENMASTER

TOWER OF LONDON, UK

Be kind to the Tower's unkindness of ravens.

In this role, you're one of 37 Yeoman Warders, or Beefeaters, at the Tower of London... and the only Ravenmaster. You need to maintain the health of the ravens (a group of these birds is called an unkindness!) that call the Tower home, because, according to legend, if the ravens should leave the Tower, it will crumble and great harm will befall the kingdom.

CAW!

The Ravenmaster has this special crest on his Yeoman Warder's tunic.

Your job is to feed and care for the ravens. They live in enclosures within the Tower walls but are free to roam during the day. The birds don't usually fly far, but they may occasionally wonder what life is like outside and so you need to keep your eyes on them. You'll also conduct tours of the Tower, a royal palace that was once an infamous prison. Of course, visitors will want to know about the birds!

To get this unique job, you'll need to become a Yeoman Warder first. To do this, you must have at least 22 years of military service and have earned a good-conduct medal. You'll then undergo a five-year apprenticeship with the current Ravenmaster before you can take over the role. And even after waiting 27 years minimum... it's the ravens that get the deciding vote—they'll definitely show whether they like you or not!

The ravens can make a variety of noises.

JOB INFO:

HAZARDS: Occasional pecks from the birds.

BONUS: You'll live in a house within the Tower walls.

EXTRA TASKS: Run a social media account to keep the world updated on the ravens.

Ravens are intelligent birds—they like to steal potato chips from tourists and bury their treasure!

A DAY IN THE LIFE OF
A RAVENMASTER

The current Ravenmaster, Chris Skaife, has been in the role for over a decade and feels like a proud parent as he looks after the seven raven residents, plus brand-new babies! To secure the future of his feathered friends (and the kingdom!), Chris oversees the Tower of London's very successful breeding program.

6am The day starts at first light as Chris lets the ravens out and cleans their cages. Luckily, he lives within the Tower walls, so he doesn't have a long commute to work.

7am Breakfast for the birds is a special diet of meats, including mice, and the occasional boiled egg. If the birds are lucky, they'll also get some blood-soaked cookies. The blood comes from the local meat market—not the ancient heads of kings and queens that were cut off when the Tower acted as a jail!

2pm For the ravens to breed, they like peace, quiet, and privacy. Chris spends lots of time making sure the birds are comfortable inside their enclosures and have all the twigs, fluff, and straw they need to build a nest.

4pm Four raven chicks hatched in 2019, and once they were old enough to leave their parents, Chris looked after them at home. The Ravenmaster needs to form a special bond with the birds, so it's important to treat them like family. Chris then selected a chick called George to live at the Tower permanently, and George gets special attention to make sure he grows into a firm friend and resident.

The Tower's ravens all have tags on their legs.

8pm As night falls, Chris will whistle a special note to call the ravens home and then safely puts them to bed in their spacious cages.

GOOD TO KNOW

The birds are free to fly during the day but need to be kept secure at night to avoid any unwanted attacks by predatory foxes.

The resident ravens are Erin, Poppy, Merlina, Jubilee, Harris, Gripp, Rocky, and now baby George.

Circus PERFORMER

Express yourself in a unique way.

Do you want to run away and join the circus? You'll travel around with colleagues who will become like family, and put on a show to blow the socks off your audience. All you need is a special skill and a wish to dress up and perform over and over again.

You'll probably be paid per show, and you'll get more if your act is unique.

There are three main types of circus shows. First is the "big top" tour, where you, the stage, and even the chairs travel around the world for 11 months of the year. People come to watch the show in the specially made tent, and you'll perform on around 300 nights of the year.

Tip: Build up your confidence by performing during a parade or local event.

Each year, around 10 million people enjoy the awesome displays of Cirque Medrano—a French traveling circus.

90

Another type of circus is the arena tour, where you also move between cities but perform in local theaters or stadiums instead of a tent. You may need to adapt your set to fit the stage size or learn how to work with the equipment available, and so these tours typically perform around 270 times a year.

An arena show put on by Ringling Bros. and Barnum & Bailey.

Finally, there's the resident circus show. You'll set up in one location (Las Vegas is popular), and your audience travels to see you. Because the set is ready and waiting, you may perform between 380 and 470 times a year—that's more than once a day on quite a few days of the year!

All you need to do to join the circus is attend an audition and show off your skills. But to have the best chance against your talented competition, think about joining a circus school like Circomedia in the UK or the Flying Fruit Fly Circus in Australia for some training. Here, you'll learn how to juggle, fire twirl, tightrope walk, unicycle, and swing on a trapeze, as well as how to become a clown.

Circus school is hard work but lots of fun!

A DAY IN THE LIFE OF
A CIRCUS ACROBAT

To be the best, you'll want to perform with one of the world's most famous circus companies. They put on shows that feature amazing acrobatic skills and colorful characters. Most circuses will offer a professional contract for a year if you pass the auditions at their headquarters.

Warm up your muscles before trying the most extreme poses.

8am As an acrobat, you are working your body all day every day, so a good night's sleep is important. Wake up gently then have a healthy, but light, breakfast.

9am Head straight to the gym for a morning warm-up. If you're injured, you won't be able to perform, so stretching and easing into your day of exercise is the most important part of your preparation for the show. Now is also the time to tweak your moves—there's always room for improvement.

12pm Time for a rehearsal on stage. This is particularly important if you're performing in a new venue. It's where you meet up with your fellow acrobats and see how they are feeling so you can adjust as a team if needed.

1pm The afternoon gives you a chance to rest, but then you need to start applying your stage makeup! There are so many performers in the circus that lots of makeup artists are on hand to help. Remember to eat your main meal of the day now so you'll be fueled up for the show.

10pm The whole circus is full of energy after a show so the gang gets together for some exercise to slowly warm down and chill out before bed.

8pm The curtain rises and you're on! Circus acrobats do their own number but also help to change the scenery or support others during their routine, so it's a nonstop couple of hours.

GOOD TO KNOW

Sometimes you may have an afternoon show as well as an evening show. Eat lots of protein to keep your muscles growing.

Professional MERMAID

Set your mermaid spirit free.

Become a mermaid and not only will you spend your working days in the water, but you'll also be an ambassador for the planet's beautiful oceans. Professional mermaids swim in live or filmed productions and can be hired for special events like birthday parties or photo shoots. You can be a mermaid or a merman!

These half-human, half-fish creatures of the sea have been written about since ancient times and are known for their mesmerizing songs. How is your singing voice?

Mermen are the male counterparts to female mermaids.

Team up with a fellow mermaid and create a synchronized swimming routine.

Picture credits

The publisher would like to thank the following for their kind permission to reproduce their photographs:
(Key: a-above; b-below; c-centre; f-far; l-left; r-right; t-top)

Alamy: Andrey Nekrasov 6 (c), Everett Collection Inc 9 (c), Martin Florin Emmanuel 10 (b), Stefano Paterna 12 (r), Ulrich Doering 15 (b), Stephen Barnes 26 (bc), Goldyrocks 26 (tr), AF archive 27 (tr), TCD/Prod.DB 36, TCD/Prod.DB 37 (c), RGB Ventures 37 (b), age fotostock 38, Tanguy de Saint Cyr 48, Nature Picture Library 49 (b), Steve Fisher 50 (cr), Montgomery Martin 51 (tr), dpa picture alliance archive 59 (br), Richard Levine 64, Eric Carr 65 (c), Neil Setchfield 67 (cl, tr), DavidCC 67 (br), VCG 69 (tr), Disney Magic 69 (c), John Warburton-Lee Photography 70 (t), John Warburton-Lee 71 (b), Southmind 76 (bc), Oleg Nikishin 77 (b), Richard Levine 80 (bc), wunkley 81 (tr), Design Pics Inc 81 (br), Lucas Vallecillos 82 (r), myLAM 82 (c), Finnbarr Webster Editorial 90 (bl), Randy Duchaine 91 (tr), Images-USA 95 (t)

ASL Airlines/James Cahill: 74 (c, t)

Dreamstime: Xi Zhang back cover (b), Xi Zhang 4 (l), Xi Zhang 4 (c), Chatchadaporn Kittisaratham 7 (l), Danny Raustadt 8 (c), Danny Raustadt 9 (r), Danny Raustadt (b), Olga0000oni 10 (t), Kampwit 11 (c), Matthijs Kuijpers 11 (b), Jocrebbin 14 (cl), Oleksándr Bondarenko 14 (br), Dirk De Keyser 15 (tr), Alena Redchanka 16 (tr), Xalanx 16 (l), Guarant 17 (tr), Rafael Ben Ari 17 (cl), Volodymyr Byrdyak 17 (b), Feng Cheng 18 (t), Quietbits 19 (cr), Massimo Parisi 19 (cr), Iuliia Ariukh 19 (bl), Gary Perkin 20, Anastasia Yakovleva 21 (tl), Pashok 21 (c), Vadymvdrobot 22 (bc), Tea 23 (tr), Artzzz 23 (tl), Vadim Zakharishchev 27 (bl), Maxim Lupascu 41 (cr), Mikhail Makeev 43 (b), Dimitar Lazarov 50 (tl), Dimarik16 50 (bl), Feverpitched 51 (c), Zyzybilo 61 (c), Jiawangkun 65 (c), Karen Foley 65 (b), Showface 70 (b), Yongyut Chanthaboot 71 (t), Belish 75 (c), Phillip Danze 75 (t), Ukrphoto 76 (t), Ponsulak 79 (c), Wavebreakmediamicro 84 (c), Dmytro Skrypnykov 84 (b), Pojoslaw 84 (b), Speedfighter17 90 (t), Fotostraveller 91 (br), Max-Ferrero/Sync (bc), Wrangel 91 (c, cl), Irina Kharchenko 94 (bc), Izanbar 95 (c, b), Nina Lisitsyna (throughout), Ian Andreiev (throughout)

Getty Images: Roger Ressmeyer back cover (l), 4 (l), Saul Loeb 2 (t), VCG 4 (t), China Photos 5, Rodrigo Arangua/AFP 13 (c, t), Daniel Leal-Olivas 21 (bl), The Washington Post 24 (l), Matt Cardy 25 (br), The Asahi Shimbun 39 (t, c), Steve Snowden 43 (cl), Wolfgang Kaehler 44 (tr), Roger Ressmeyer/Corbis/VCG 46 (bc, tr), KONTROLAB 47 (b), ROMEO GACAD/AFP 49 (t), Anadolu Agency 52 (t), Los Angeles Times 52 (t), Universal Images Group 53 (b), Los Angeles Times 53 (c), Paul Harris 53 (tr), Jane Barlow - PA Images 56 (bc), AFP 60 (t), Dan Istitene 61 (b), Hoch Zwei 61 (c), Saul Loeb 64 (t), Jamie McCarthy 64 (bc), Petit Philippe 66 (bc), Brett Hemmings 68 (t), TORSTEN BLACKWOOD/AFP 72, Universal Images Group 73 (bl), TORSTEN BLACKWOOD/AFP 73 (c), dotshock 73 (b), Murray Close 77 (c), ALEXANDER NEMENOV/ AFP 77 (t), Gamma-Rapho 78 (t), Wolfgang Kaehler 79 (tr),

LightRocket 80 (t), Keystone 83 (tl), LightRocket 83 (br), Jack Taylor 87 (t), ullstein bild 94 (t)

LEGOLAND®: Jonathan Hordle/ INhouse images back cover (r), 18 (bl), Jonathan Hordle/INhouse images 19 (tl), 20 (bc), 21 (bc, b)

Lonely Planet Images: James Gulliver Hancock 32, James Gulliver Hancock 34-35 (all images), 41 (br)

Monterey Bay Aquarium: 6 (r), 7 (r)

NASA Images: 54 (bl), 55 (b, t), 56-57 (all except main)

Sand in Your Eye: 28-29 (all images), 78 (bc), 79 (br, bl)

Shutterstock: stockcreations 1 (c), AJR_photo 1 (r), Dmitrii Larusov 2 (b), vectorsicon.com 8 (c), S.Jeshurun Vineeth Roshan 11 (t), Inspired By Maps 13 (b), Olinchuk 14 (tr), Four Oaks 15 (tl), Yuliya Artiukh 15 (tc), Louis.Roth 22 (tr), Standret 23 (br), Africa Studio 23 (r), Tony Moran 23 (bl), sirtravelalot 24 (bc), Kozlik 25 (cl, tr), Creativa Images 27 (cl), Lakeview Images 27 (br), Chaosamran_Studio 33 Luciana Carla Funes 37 (t), Mark Agnor 39 (br), FrameStockFootages 40 (bc), Leonel Calara 40 (t), PIYAWAT WONGOPASS 41 (tr), Dianov Boris 42, Thomas Barrat 43 (t), Vlad G 44 (bl), Jaroslav Moravcik 45 (tl), Puwadol Jaturawutthichai 45 (cl), paleontologist natural 45 (cr), AKKHARAT JARUSILAWONG 45 (b), Linnas 47 (t), sirtravelalot 47 (c), Dmitry Kalinovsky 51 (br), Triff 52 (c), Castleski 54 (tr), Gorodenkoff 58 (t, bc), Rawpixel. com 59 (c), Africa Studio 59 (tr), Hafiz Johari 60 (bl), ntotlyar 62 (t), Alpa Prod 62 (bc), Alpa Prod 63 (tr), Africa Studio 63 (bl), Grafvision 63 (c), stockcreations 63 (bc), Andy Dean Photography 63 (br), grafvision 66 (t), Travelling Homebodies 67 (bl), Dmitrii Iarusov 68 (bc), GregD 69 (br), Anastasia Myasnikova 71 (c), Leonard Zhukovsky 75 (b), NPS_87 81 (c), 2p2play 82 (bl), nd3000 85 (b), Iakov Filimonov 85 (c), AboutLife 85 (tr), Anton Ivanov 87 (c), RZ Images 92, ID1974 93 (b), CREATISTA 93 (t), Miloje (throughout), Giamportone (throughout)

Space Invaders: TAITO 1978 41 (l)

The London Dungeon: 30-31 (all images)

Tower of London: 86 (all images), 87 (br), 88-89 (all images)

To become a professional mermaid you should attend a mermaid workshop. You'll spend time learning about your equipment, safety, and how to move gracefully in the water. Real mermaids can breathe underwater, but as you're still human, you'll need to master free-diving techniques so you can hold your breath safely for longer. This training will allow you to work at events that could make you an income of $47,000 a year.

Mermaids swim by rolling their hips for movement. They don't use their arms or fins!

The most important piece of equipment you need to invest in is your tail. A monofin is covered with colorful mermaid skin made out of fabric or rubber, and costs between a few hundred and a few thousand dollars.

GOOD TO KNOW

So much time in the water may irritate your eyes and ear canals, and having your human feet bound into the tail can cause blisters. Look after these areas when you are back on dry land.

ROLE MODELS

Look up these professional mermaids:
Mermaid Linden, California
Mermaid Kat, Perth, Australia
The Mermaids at Weeki Wachee Springs, Florida